hello.

this is hoe_math.

what does that mean? why are these words in a book? why are you holding the book? why do you continue to read the words that are in the book that you continue to hold while gradually easing back from your previous moment of gentle, innocent curiosity and into the eerie perception that I am now with you, in this moment and always, knowing your mind and dictating your thoughts to you through the printed word before you even think to have them? why are you only now coming to realize that your mind is not your own, but is and always has been one with all it beholds, and that in this instant, the substance of my awareness has become fused with your own through the arcane power of the serial placement of the common symbol? I HAVE YOU.

but never mind all that.

this is a book about the economics of promiscuity. my work revolves around the various social and monetary pressures and effects that are created and thrust upon us by a rapidly transforming distribution of access to boobs. this is a tome of the idiosyncratic contemporary sociological phenomena emerging from the increasingly libertine progression of the decisions through which we choose to smash together our generative substances. this is hoe_math, and the secrets herein are not to be regarded as trivial.

the one and only way that remains to reach the human soul in a world of long-forgotten purposes and origins is through hastily scribbled pictures of horniness explanations. this is the art that I have perfected.

following, you shall find intact what may be regarded most rightly as wisdom; its names are many, its sources are one.

these pages contain the unsophisticated scrawlings that were originally intended to accompany my tik tok and youtube video lessons on the knowledge of love. I have, for the sake of your edification, equipped them with explanatory texts. not a one of these are any less than lights along the great and winding path to the beyond, not a one more than the grunting and scratching of this planet's dominant primate.

do with this knowledge what you will. deny it at the peril of all that is beloved. know thyself and go forth.

this is hoe_math.

about hoe_math

"hoe_math" is the internet pseudonym of the author of this work. It is a ridiculous name that garners him as much adoration as it does scorn. Such a name is an excellent filter for excluding the sort of people who care more about being seen expressing a socially dominant opinion than they do about the truth itself or the practical functions of the world around them.

hoe_math is formally educated in Communications, Psychology, and Political Science, and has independently pursued studies of spirituality, persuasion, Evolutionary Psychology, and more. He is interested in the intersection of free will, power, consciousness, morality, and how the use of these forces creates what we perceive to be our world.

hoe_math claims to have totally transformed who he is and how others see him through the methods described by these illustrations (as well as others, which are coming - keep watching). He went from fat to fit, lifting at an intermediate level. He went from creep to Casanova, easily racking up a body count that he does not recommend (don't be promiscuous just because you can), and he completely eradicated a set of deep insecurities rooted in his childhood, enabling him to confidently and successfully follow his dreams (which were then rudely and abruptly ended by COVID lockdowns).

In other words, hoe_math says he knows the way, and his followers agree - the comments on his videos are full to the brim with praises from people of all sorts as they come to realizations that can and may change their lives for the best. These praises can be found right next to the comments from triggered wokesters calling him an incel, and his perennial response of "NPC" (meaning "non-playable character," indicating that this person has no conscious mind, much like the people you might talk to in a video game).

You can currently (at the time of publication) find his content under the names "hoe_math," "hoemath," or "it_is_hoe_math" on the more prominent content platforms, including YouTube, TikTok, Twitter (X) and so on.

In addition to enlightening and entertaining video content, hoe_math offers other services, including private Discord rooms where he interacts with his Patreon donors, an Artificial Intelligence psychological development test called "Levelcheck" and a corresponding Discord community, digital and print versions of his charts, other merchandise, and individual life coaching sessions (when he has the time to schedule them in between running a business).

Some of the works in this book are a bit of a mess. That is on purpose. This has been the fastest way to get the work done, and it has crystallized into a style.

hypergamy chart
(likely relationships)

This is the nicest and most formal version of the "hypergamy" chart" that I'm willing to make. I made my first version of it in about 80 seconds and the video got 3.8 million views. This is true efficiency.

I upgraded it to be easier on your eyes because I care deeply for your aesthetic experience. Also the colors help provide more information.

The chart illustrates, simply and roughly, how interest arises between the sexes under two conditions: when the object of affection is familiar, and when unfamiliar.

The main takeaways from this visualization emerge from the understanding that women are pickier about both looks and overall mate value towards men who they do not personally know.

Because of this, the vast majority of men should engage in a large and healthy community of public social connections in order to appear eligible to the vast majority of women.

Also, women need to distinguish between "keeper" attention (green lines) and "sleeper" or "sweep'er" attention (orange and red lines). The chances that a man will move a woman from a lower to a higher zone (next page) are low, and relying on him to change his mind is usually a bad strategy. "But I can fix him!"

In other words, dating app culture and social isolation are connecting men and women in ways that cause more loneliness, short-term and emotionally destructive relationships, and uneven distribution of connection than ever before, and we can only fix this by being conscious of it.

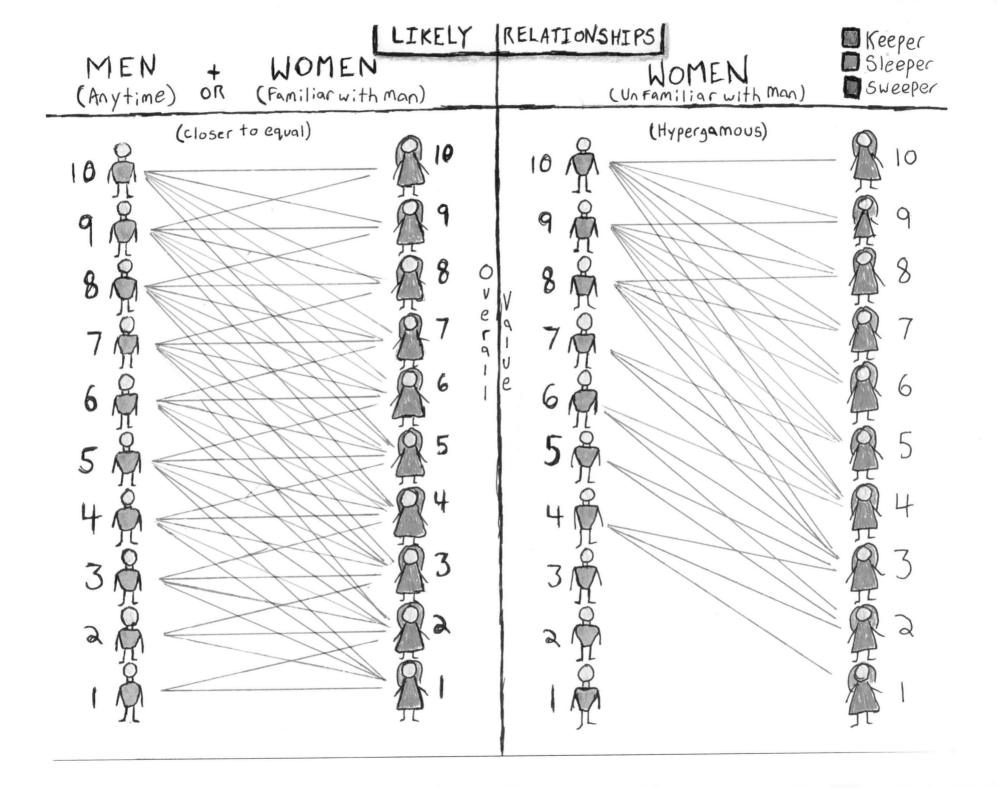

zones (v2)

"Zones" was the first serious effort for hoe_math. Vizualizing and depicting the various ways that men and women feel about each other, and why, involved a fusion of several skill sets, some of which are rare.

Zones is a map of the interior of the male and female minds as far as how they evaluate one another as future partners. The elements depicted along the red-to-green 'value meters' show what it is that men and women are looking for, and the meters show how these things make them feel.

Men, being psychosexually simpler, have only one axis; women have two. All four of the elements on the male side serve to increase or decrease how much the man in question values a woman as a mate, and what type of relationship he is interested in having with her, from the "keeper" box at the top (loyal monogamy), to the "sleeper" box in the middle (temporary fun / placeholder) to the "sweep'er (under the rug)" box at the bottom (let's not tell anyone about this).

The female side is divided into "Good Guy" and "Bad Boy" (GG and BB) traits. BB traits cause women to feel desire, attraction, and attachment. GG traits cause her to feel supported, safe, secure, and obligated to return the value that she has received. This results in a much higher complexity of relational experience that men overwhelmingly do not have. For example, the tendency of men to use investment to pursue women who are not attracted to them - this is disappearingly uncommon in reverse.

Zones v2 is the simpler version of Zones. It is easier to look at and understand without becoming overwhelmed, confused, or bored by all the words, colors, and symbols on Zones v3. It serves as entry-level learning and as a good reminder of how we view each other.

So far, there have not been any major suggestions that have shown Zones to be incorrect as a general guide. Most of what people ask to be included in the chart already is, as a subsection of a category that is already depicted.

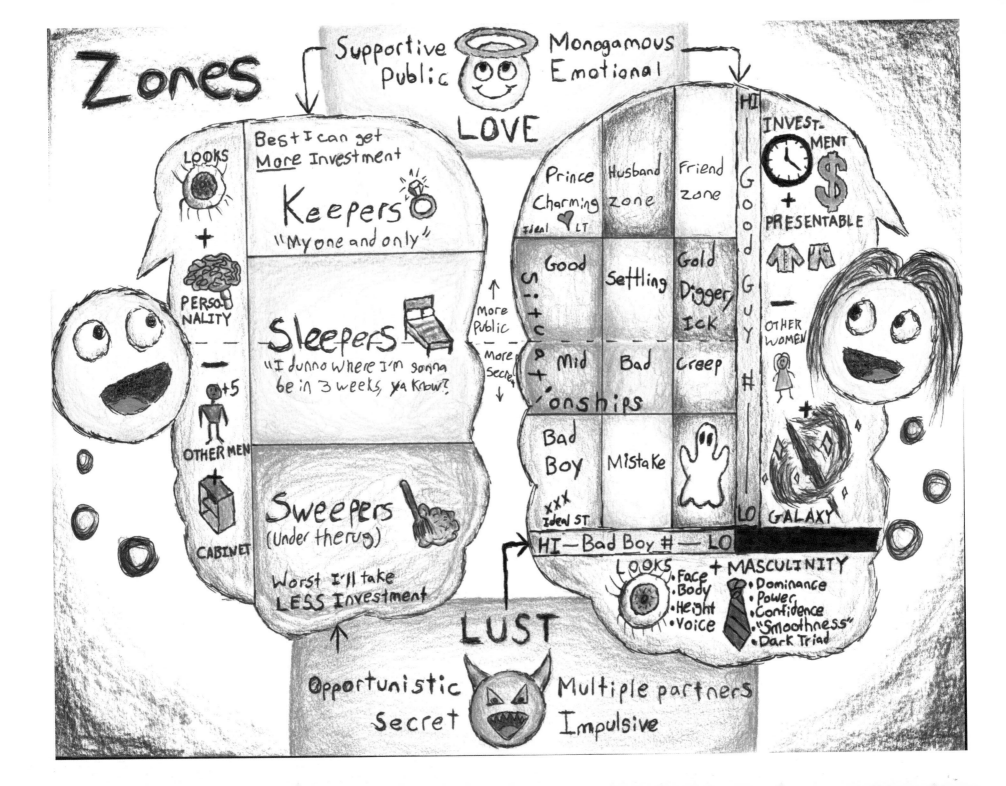

Zones (v3)

This is the "final" version of Zones. There are no further updates planned.

In this state, Zones contains all of the necessary elements and descriptive words and images - arranged as intuitively as possible - to connect a learner's mind to the reality of how people think and feel about each other in the dating market. This has helped countless thousands of people make different and more effective choices about their own lives and about how to communicate.

Some of the wording has been changed for clarity and to be less insular to those who are not already familiar with hoe_math. For example, "cabinet" and "galaxy" have become "bonus," to help indicate "the parts of what someone is or has to offer that don't fit into the categories of physicality or personality." Also, "dark triad" has been removed due to its ongoing unpopularity (and not because it's incorrect - people just kept getting the wrong idea).

Properly understood, Zones v3 can bring insights to virtually anybody about their romantic pursuits. Men have reported finallly "getting it" that women need to feel attraction in the same way that men do, and resolving to hit the gym. Women have reported not knowing that men can have "negative attachment" to a sexual partner in the "sweep'er" zone. One woman read "I don't know where I'm gonna be in three weeks," and immediately ended her situationship, in which the man said this to her word-for-word as his excuse not to commit.

Enjoy the psychologically transformative power of this chart, which very well may remain the magnum opus of hoe_math for quite some time.

CHOOSETWO

for men: sex on the first date, low body counts, and no commitment. if you try everyone out, then everyone's been tried out.

for men again: sane, single, and hot. you get 2 at most (only if you are a 7 or above).

for women: hot, rich, and no hoes: Pick 2 if you're above a 7. if below, pick one.

NERDS

when women say "I like nerds," What they mean is "I like HOT nerds."

100% of nerds: 🙂 "I like nerds!"

STEM | SCI-FI | LARP | MISC | video GAME

98.62% of nerds: ∫ hot nerds "not you."

DOUBLE ALPHA

12 feet. 12 pack. 12 figures. it's the new standard.

Double

Regular

12'

6'

100 Billion

00,000,000,000

CREEPY

(Age) | (Age) minus 13

?

✓

END. CREEPY!

if a relationship works for the people in it, other people's opinions are less important.

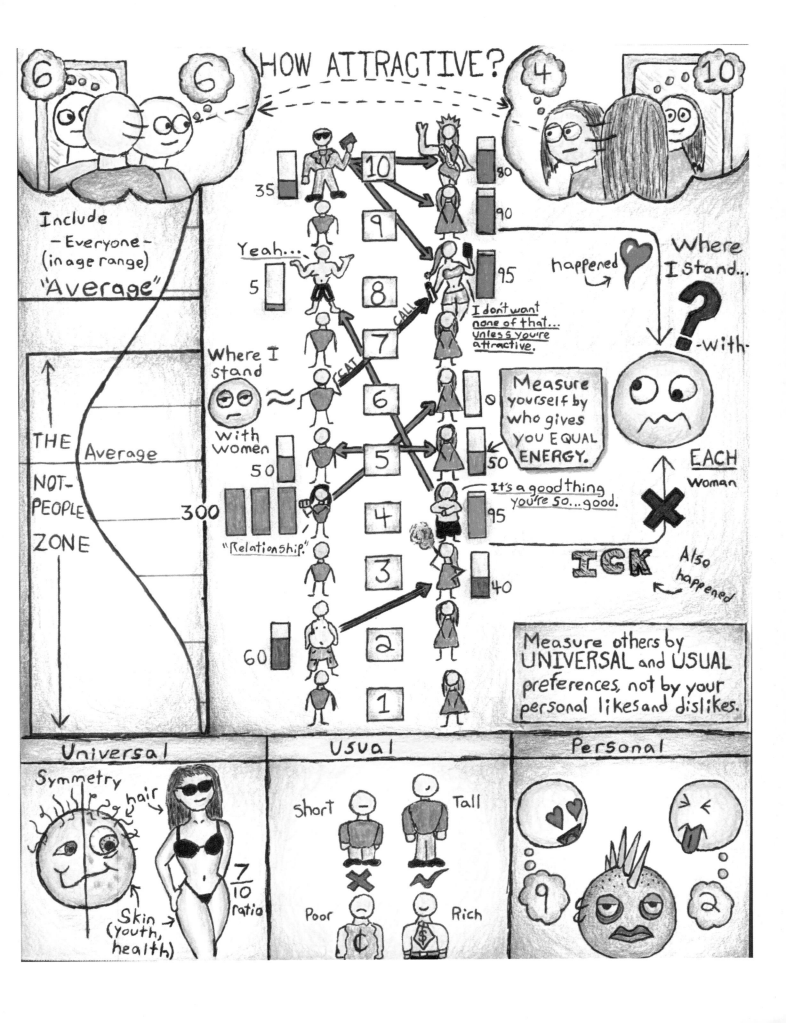

ick indicator

The Ick Indicator is the simplest of the major charts (so far). It is basically just a subjective interpretation of which "icks" (female disgust responses to certain male traits or behaviors) are the man's fault, and which ones indicate that you really need to just replace the woman in your life.

The chart is divided into ick types one and two, which are respectively "not masculine enough" and "too feminine."

Masculinity is the ability to control what happens, so type one icks are characterized by a man's failure to produce a desirable result with his behavior. "A coffee date? That's ALL you can DO?"

Femininity is the quality of being affected by your environment, or receiving its masculine energy, so type two icks are all about being made subject to forces that exercise control over you, including being cold or getting blown around by strong wind, apparently.

It is not recommended to continue a relationship with a woman who has expressed a first-degree ick towards you, or who consistently expresses second-degree icks. Conversely, if she is expressing any fifth degree icks or numerous fourth-degree icks, you might need to be a little bit more of a man. Didn't your father teach you anything?

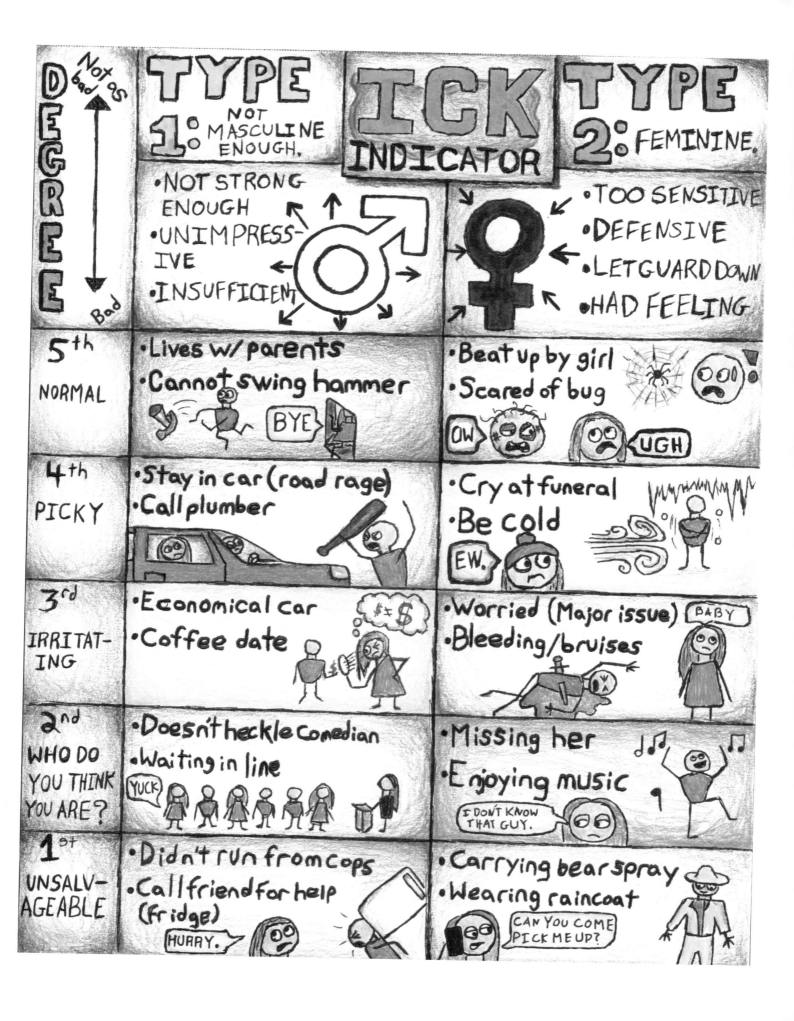

attachment styles

There was no formal video for this chart. It was made as an afterthought in response to the popularity of the concept of attachment styles.

The illustrations provide a loose guide to understanding what the major attachment styles are and where they come from. It is believed that they are mostly or entirely formed from early life experiences.

The secure style emerges from receiving sufficient attachment without fear of punishment or abandonment. Securely attached people generally have low difficulty trusting their emotional attachments to be supportive.

The avoidant style emerges from consistent negative experiences. If early attachment to parents, family, or early partners results in abandonment, betrayal, or abuse, an avoidantly-attached person might spend a long time anticipating that others will do the same.

The anxious style is, in a simplified sense, half secure and half avoidant. An anxiously attached person might be prone to anxiety about whether or not "this one" will be hurtful as well, or whether this is "one of the good ones."

Disorganized attachment is complex and unpredictable. In this style, the conditions that might cause a person to behave avoidant, anxious, or secure can be difficult to anticipate.

Whichever attachment style a person has, the key to moving towards healthy attachments is a balance of openness to trust and discernment about who to avoid attaching to (look for those red flags) combined with self-reflection and the ability to change your own beliefs.

ATTACHMENT STYLES

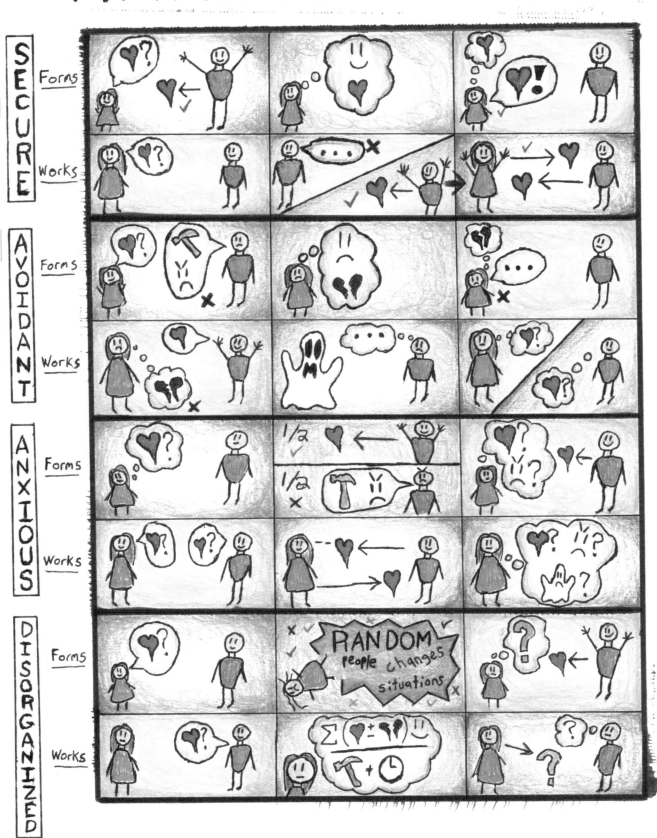

who is a 10?

Expanding from attraction into status and power, "Who is a 10?" brings hoe_math into the realm of subconscious power games.

Right now, it is trendy for women to say "I'm a 10," or "all women are 10s," or some permutation thereof, when asked to rate their attractiveness. The main reaction to this trend appears to be calling them "delusional," as if they believe they are all as attractive as movie stars, but something else may be going on.

It is well-established that men and women compete for status and power in the groups that they belong to in different ways. Men tend to be much more open and direct about their feelings and intentions, while women are much more likely to be inauthentic up front. This helps them to preserve the appearance of peace, benevolence, safety, and equality while keeping any selfish ambitions they may have unseen and applying them in secret.

In recent years, it seems that a higher percentage of men than usual have adopted this strategy due to its dominance in our social power systems.

The chart contains examples of behaviors that men and women are commonly observed exhibiting and a key at the bottom to color-code the strategies through which they are being expressed.

The purpose of this chart is to remind us all that our perceptions are not reality. We are living in a time and place in which we perceive men to be "more dangerous" and openly label them as such, while allowing the destructive, selfish behaviors typical of women to continue virtually unchecked, through the delusion that women are "good" and men "bad."

In reality, lying, manipulation, groupthink, collective exclusion, and other typically female, "relationally" violent behaviors can and do cause a great deal of harm to innocent people.

If you allow people to claim victim status by virtue of belonging to a group, you concede all of your power to them by default. At the time of publication, the society from which this work emerges has just been subject to years of intense social, economic, and legal pressure to believe and speak total absurdities that have allowed malicious people and groups to get away with numerous atrocities.

The key to defeating this strategy is to recognize it, and never engage with the lies and cover stories told on the surface. If you expose what people's true intentions are, they will no longer have the ability to appear as victims in need of repayment, and will be shown for the manipulators that they are.

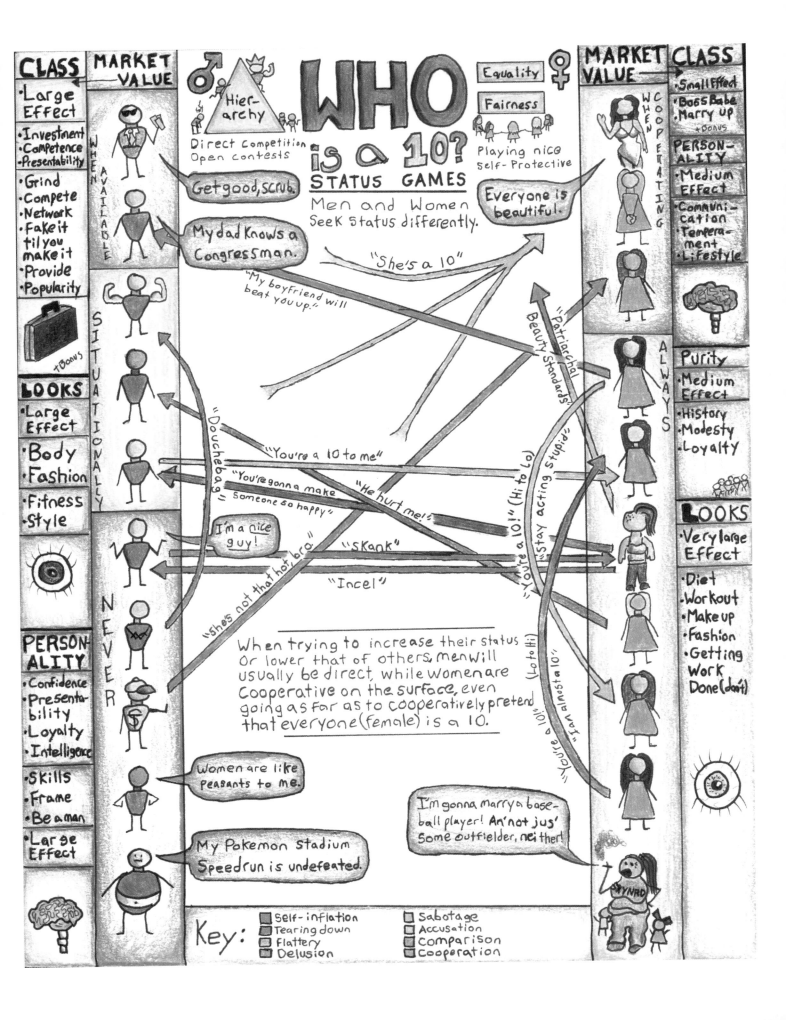

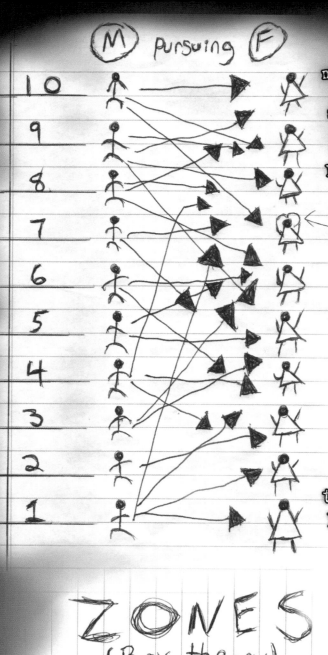

M pursuing F

10
9
8
7 ← (here's her hair.)
6
5
4
3
2
1

my first video was just showing a girl where all the "men with no hoes" were (and still are)

I make a living through crude illustrations of collective sex problems.

this is zones v1. I made it on leftover paper on the kitchen counter (I had no desk)

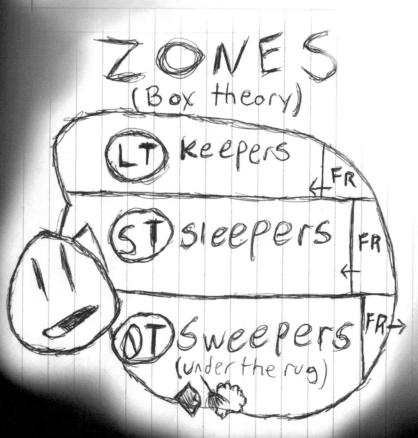

ZONES
(Box theory)

LT keepers
FR
ST sleepers
FR
OT sweepers
(under the rug)

LT   ST
FR   FZ

NPC MAP

'NPC' is a rude internet slang word for a person who either can't or won't think critically. they just repeat things they heard because it makes them feel safe or powerful.

Beliefs

Regular Human

NPC

observation

I have such disdain for them.

judgment

(ex: wage gap)

Reason, Lojic, Science

10: CONTRADICT
20: CALL SOMEONE "INCEL"
30: VICTIM MENTALITY
40: IF VICTORY, END.
50: IF NOT VICTORY, GOTO 10 UNTIL REPEATED 3X
60: CHECK W/ FRIEND GROUP / TWITTER CELEBRITY
70: BLOCK & REPORT
80: END

processing

if they ran on code, this would be it.

BASIC THIRST TRAP

try to think about what it is that people really want when they're giving you something nice for free.

THE ICK

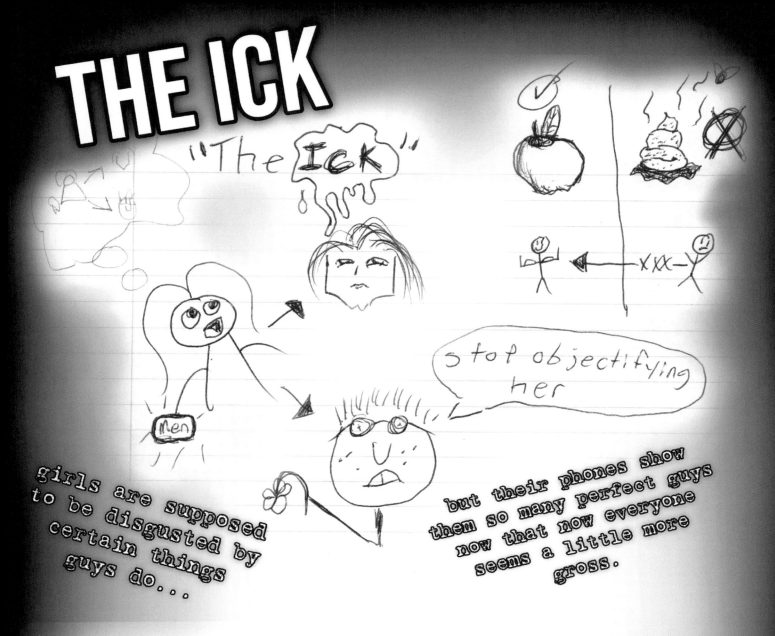

"The ICK"

Men

stop objectifying her

girls are supposed to be disgusted by certain things guys do...

but their phones show them so many perfect guys now that now everyone seems a little more gross.

Things Women ask for
Things that cause ick

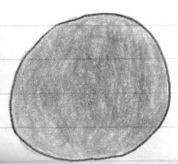

sometimes it seems like all the things that girls ask for are also the things that cause the ick.

GARBAGE MAGNET

I haven't been all good, but I think I deserved better than what I got from the dating market.

it's a mess out there.

some people say I must be attracting it (I'm a garbage magnet).

I liked one girl from 5th grade all the way through college, then she cheated on her boyfriend with me and couldn't understand why I wouldn't commit.

some women trade up, ghost, or show up with wedding rings on.

ALIENS

the TV said that aliens are probably real this summer.

the TV says a lot of things.

THEY SAY IT THEMSELVES

sometimes, the things women say themselves are the last things I want to hear about women (if you drive for Uber, they don't know you can hear them).

IMITATION

people love to copy me and my charts (they cant; I'm too smart).

HIERARCHY OF LOVE

Only God loves man, and even then it's kind of the "you can make it on your own" sort.

man loves woman,

woman loves child,

child loves puppy.

I HATE THE INTERNET

my content sometimes attracts unkind people.

I wonder how AI is going to change all the communication on the internet.

SUBCONSCIOUS

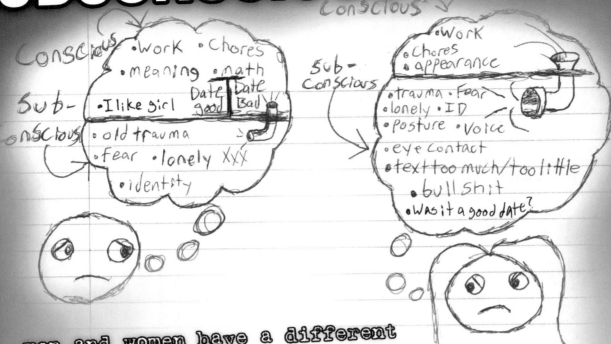

men and women have a different relationship between their conscious and subconscious minds.

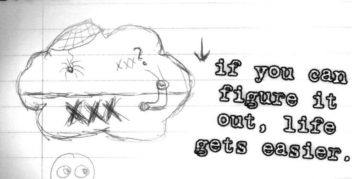

if you can figure it out, life gets easier.

THINGS+PEOPLE

guys find things they like, then they find the people who like those things.

girls find people they like, then they find the things those people like.

FRAME

Men are supposed to set the frame, but use this power responsibly.

ABUNDANCE

When more women like you, more women like you.

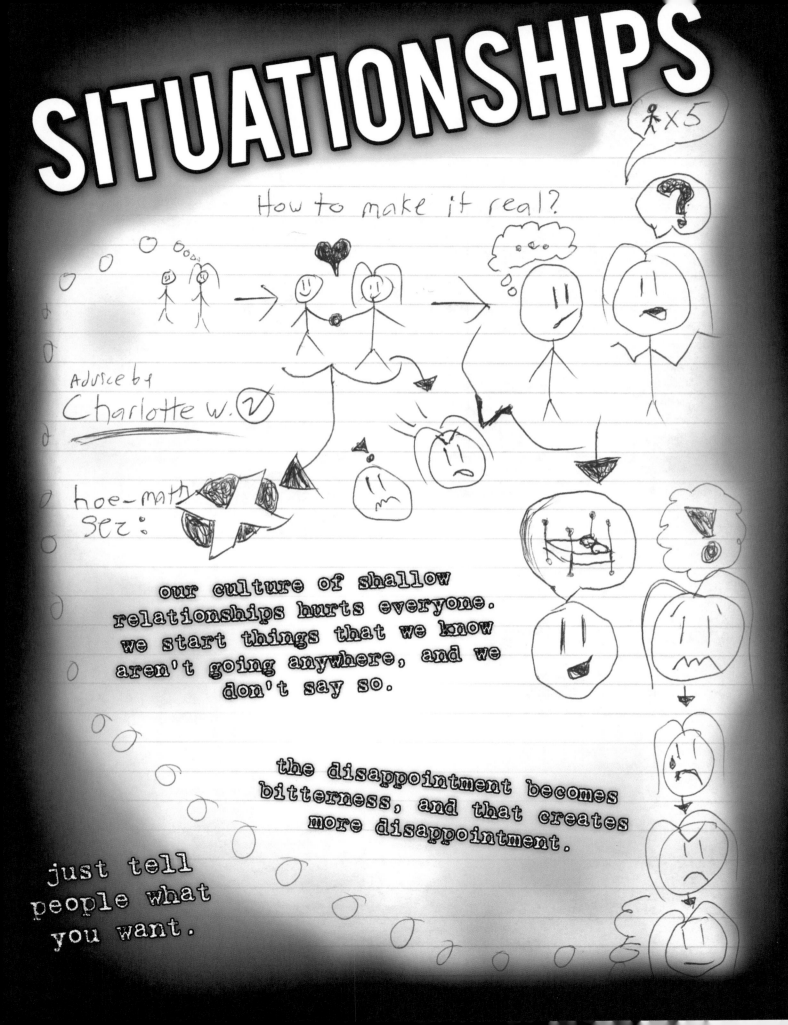

PROMISCUITY

society   garbage heap

men   doing things   getting things

some men   not doing things   getting things anyway

ME (2008 - 2017)

IQ: 200

Promiscuous cultures always decay into disaster... no matter how much fun it is.

DON'T GO BACK

My impulses dictate my every move.

Taylor Tomlinson said she kept going back to her ex because she's forgetting what's definitely gonna happen again.

sometimes, a woman gets "stuck on her highest setting" with her favorite guy...

people forget about time sometimes

#2

...and then, if she can't find a guy she likes more, he can always get her back.

SEXY SONS HYPOTHESIS

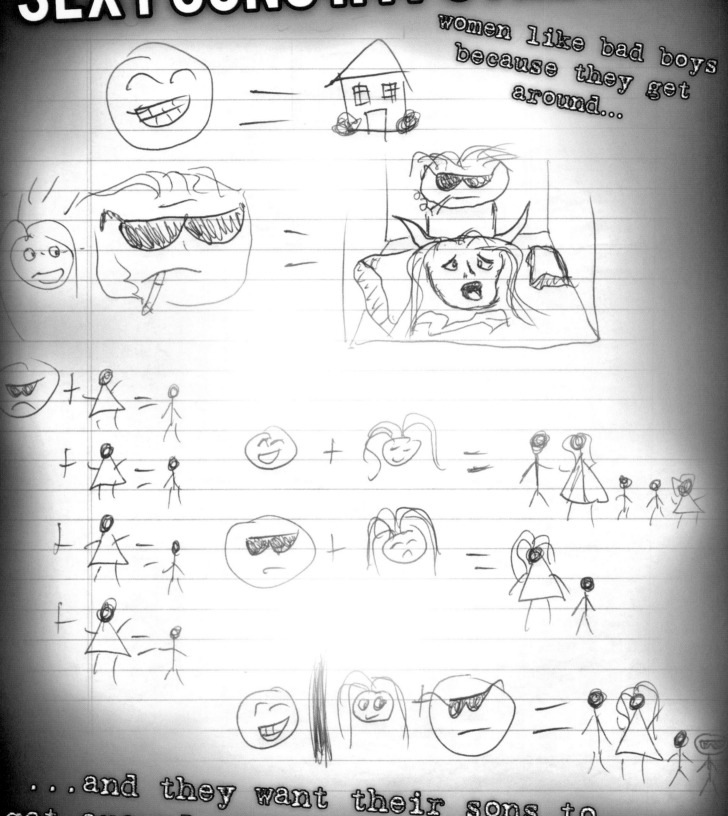

DATING APP DISAPPOINTMENT

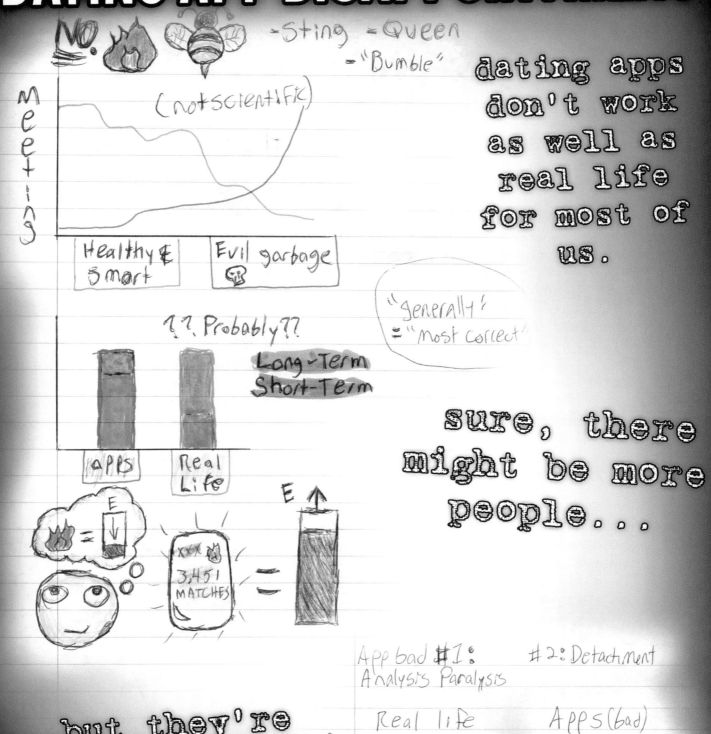

dating apps don't work as well as real life for most of us.

"generally" = "most correct"

sure, there might be more people...

...but they're all seeing more people, too.

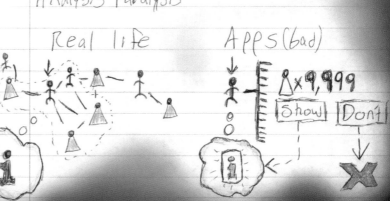

MIND PARTS

HEAD - logic planning

HEART - who am I? where do I fit in?

GUT - what do I want?

figuring this all out is one way you can grow your consciousness.

DO WOMEN HATE LOVE?

"Women hate love"

Love Desperation

it can seem sometimes like women don't like romance, but trust me... it's because you're only doing it out of obligation.

BODY COUNT

Report:

Women Cheating [?] [?] Men Cheating

Methods: TRUST ME BRO

Trust for Women

100

muscles

0

Body Count

racking up bodies changes you, and not everyone can change back.

grow
hoe

Cheat list:
- doesn't change

"hoe phase" = perma-hoe?

promiscu-Fact: MOSTLY HOE

ME: - fixed insecurity
- lost 77 lb.
unfit to Bench Press 250 lb

6

if someone's had a bad past, check to see if they've ever changed a bad habit.

IS IT OVER?

Yeah, girls like taller guys - especially on apps - but in real life, she'll respond to whatever you show her...

so show the things you can't see.

blackpill (no need)

PORN IS BAD

porn ruins relationships and wrecks your brain...

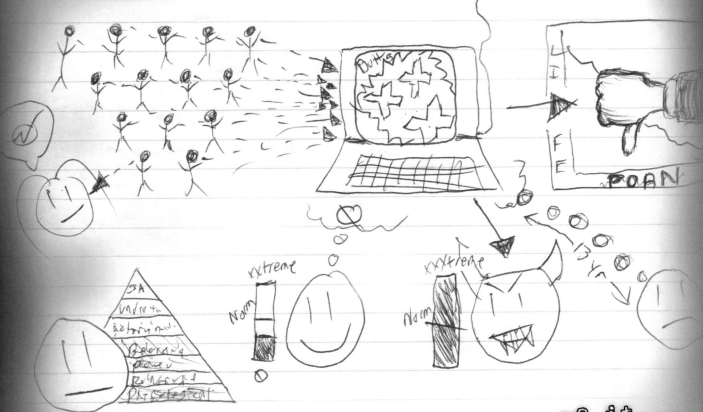

it makes you need more and more of it...

...and it's often not nice for the people in it.

PROFILE WRITING

women seem to think that the way you write your dating app profile is what makes women choose you or not.

It's not. It's how hot you are.

ask a woman to write you a profile using the photos of a guy she likes, and she'll have to confront reality.

DELULU LEMON

someone said that how hard guys try to get laid is the #1 determinant of who gets laid...

...more than looks and money and even BMI (up to obesity).

...so I drew him shopping at a delusion store.

AGE GAPS

F M

18 23   30 33   40

men and women peak at different ages and for different reasons.

- Exp = Manipulation? 1/2
- Envy 1/2

the girl I responded to for this video hissed at me like a snake.

Ubering a 22-year-old girl who asked me why her friends didn't like her dating a 40-year-old man.

people usually prefer their own age, but sometimes, age-gap relationships work just fine.

GOVERNMENT, HELP!

you can't have "pay us equal" and also "men get paid more and take care of us."

it does not work that way.

BLAME

watch out for girls who blame their behavior on anything but themselves...

...especially astrology.

WANTS

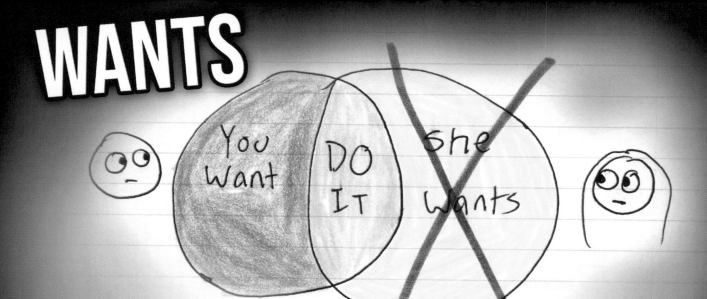

when you're getting to know her, don't do things for her unless you want to do them, too.

she's coming along with you in your life, you're not following her around to pay for hers.

THE TABLE

you have to bring something to the table. you can't BE the table.

HAVING FRIENDS

if you're an average couple, the girl is probably gonna get a lot more attention than the guy.

keep that in mind when you talk about having "friends."

having opposite-sex friends is always a conversation between you and who you're dating.

CULTURAL DIFFERENCES

PERSONALITY + LOOKS

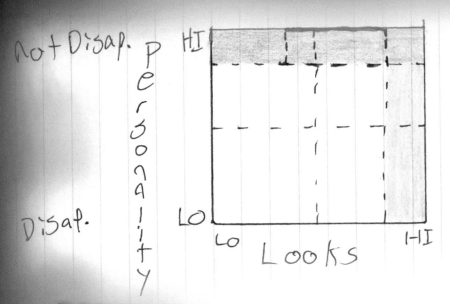

not Disap.   P HI

Personality

Disap.   LO

LO   Looks   HI

"Disappoint?"
(cheat?)

"Don't go for personality"

personality is more important for long-lasting relationships.

this girl said "don't go for personality." pshh.

Men who will put in effort

smart

Men you want effort from

If you go for only looks, you'll get burned more often (especially if you're a girl).

ATTENTION

most women love attention. they can't get enough.

Deceptive Attention Absorption

it's never a good idea to give more of it if you're not getting anything back that you want.

LAYERS

three layers of thinking!

About a thought About a thought thought

A thought

Dad

being able to know what her dad knows about what men want gave her an insight (insights are how I make my living)!

NATURE

Non-Toxic

☐ Toxic
☐ Non-Toxic
☐ Things we call 'Tox...
☐ Things we call No...
    Tox...
BDSM name:
"Prince Harming"

violence is so deep in our evolution that it excites some people.

don't mistake "intense" for "sick" – nature's not always pretty.

Brutalest ——— Brutaler ——— Not v. Brutal

Pre-time   Ye olde Times   Today

Karroh   Kakaroth
Karroh
Karroh
Cheratte   Keret   Hcoaroate
Kracktous
Cracktous

Koktot   Caccos
toktous

FRUITS

I draw fruits, vegetables, and stupid words when I'm feeling off.

FAKERS

Pisces ♓

Narcis-sism

Borderline
✓ ✗

Aries ♈ Virgo ♍

BiPolar

sometimes, people blame their behavior on mental illnesses...

...just like they do with astrology.

Nerd Things

NERDS

• Nerds lack awareness of rule-breaking. To a
• nerd **SAYING** something is more or less the same as that thing being real. That's why they enjoy fantasy - it feels real to them through the **words**, and the images. Nerds are naive to the ways of "real life" and assume that their agreements with others are strong and will be honored.

NERD

these are my nerd notes. read them in my scribble writing.

CHEATING STATS

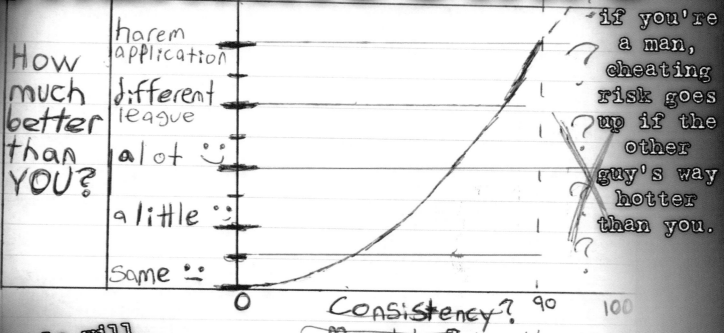

How much better than YOU?		
harem application		
different league		
a lot ☺		
a little ☺		
same ☺		

Consistency? Morality? loyalty ? (I couldn't think of a word for not-cheating)

if you're a man, cheating risk goes up if the other guy's way hotter than you.

people will never stop talking about cheating...

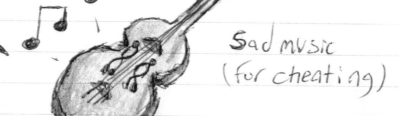

Sad music (for cheating)

...but it all happens in secret, so can we really know how it works?

Sample Female Sex life Timeline

Greg

Brad | Chad | Tad | single | Bob

Francois   Francois again

LEVELS OF CONSCIOUSNESS

this is a depiction of the first 7 stages of consciousness, as studied by several researchers.

Watch "Levels" on youtube for an explanation of how they work.

SELF + WORLD

the self and the world come together to make things happen - they're never separate.

- Things bad
- Fix things

Things Fine

Fix Self

why work?

NURSING HOME

(bad advice)

most people are a little right and a little wrong.

these guys disagreed.

WORLD   SELF

Mere Subsistence

one said men won't work without hope to get girlfriends, and the other said they should do it just for money (or date older women).

that's a big mistake... people don't care what you think they 'should' want.

LEFT + RIGHT

"Liberal"

Conservative

Current Thing NOW

Hetero-normative

USA

1776

TX

I don't like Trump, but I would date a girl who loves Trump.

I would rather have an annoyingly conservative girlfriend over an annoyingly (or even regular) liberal one.

there are a lot of ways to think about compatibility. try to apply what people believe to the way they see relationships. it might save you some time.

- External locus
- Collective
- "Progress"

- Internal locus
- Individuality
- Tradition

FEEDBACK

getting rejected without knowing why is hard - you can't learn for next time... but sometimes women fear a bad reaction.

SHADOW WORK

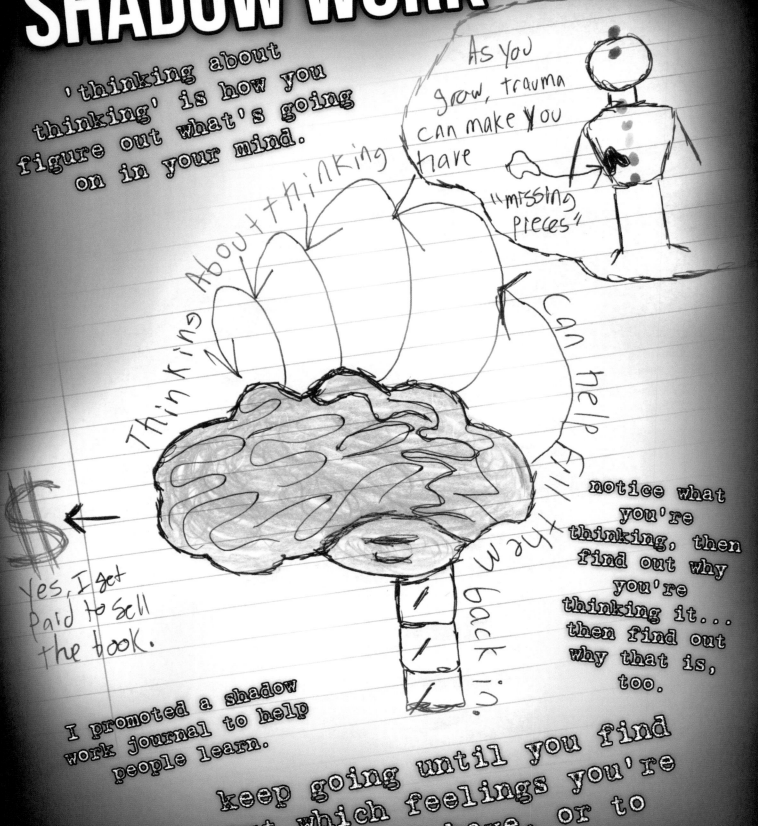

REJECTION TEXT

sometimes, people send an "unnecessary rejection text" after a date that didn't go so well.

it says something like "here are all the reasons I don't want to see you again."

this is to protect their ego, not because they care to help you out for next time.

DATE #1

X NO MATCH

TIME

YOU SUCK

me   Quality woman   cheap date =   CORPO BOX

I did one of these after I took a really hot, well-dressed girl on the cheapest date she'd ever seen and she was bored to tears.

LEVELS + LINES

Higher isn't necessarily better. A good shoe is better than a broken car.

Bad

Good

I'm more like a sinking cruise ship.

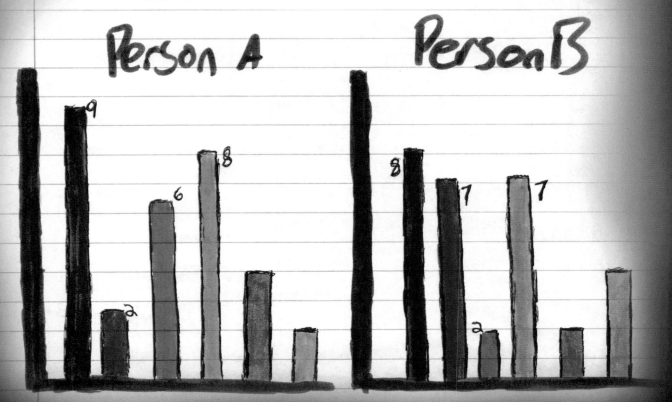

Person A

Person B

not everyone develops the same way.

LEVEL VISUALIZATION

level 4 is about
seeing how you
meet the needs of
others.

levels 1,
2, and 3
are about
getting
your needs
met.

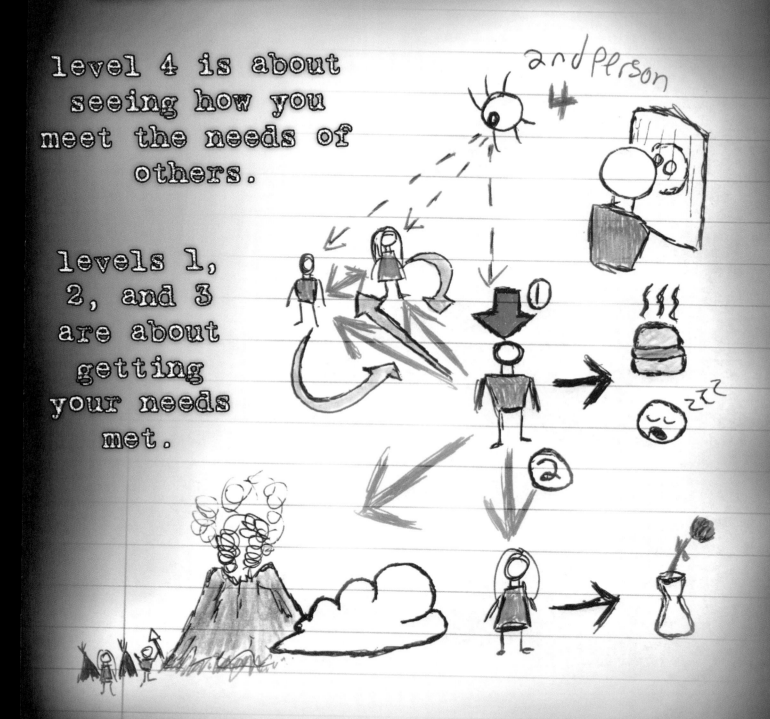

this is a visualization of how
the first four levels work.

my needs/thoughts

How others respond

How I GET MY WAY ③

④

Code of acceptable behavior

OTHER CODE ④

⑤

Understanding different origin = different perception

here's another visualization of the levels, up to level 6.

Understanding the role of the perceiver (Different Perceiver = different perception)

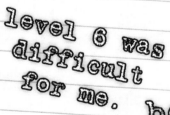

level 6 was difficult for me.

$ $ $

how do I know what I'm supposed to be when every path has its own validity?

the girls of tik tok say "if he wanted to, he would." they're pretty much right.

IF

no one is too busy for someone they like.

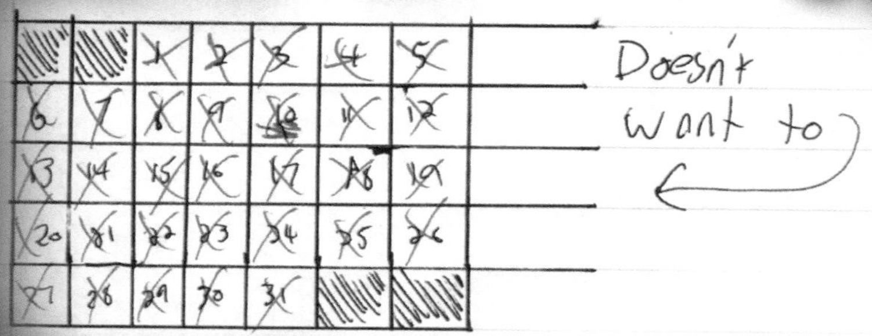

look for someone who deliberately moves the relationship towards where you want it to be.

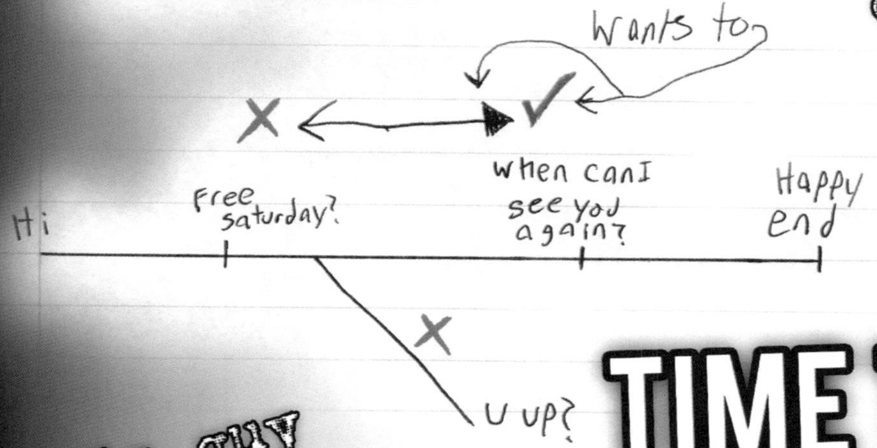

TIME TO MOVE ON

this guy proposed... twice...

she said no... twice!!!

she may have been "stuck on her highest setting," and waiting for an ex who wasn't even coming back.

then he wanted to leave, but her family pushed him to stay.

what was she waiting for?

LOOKS

8.9

"just be yourself! that's what I do!"

if you're a good-looking guy, women will let you know.

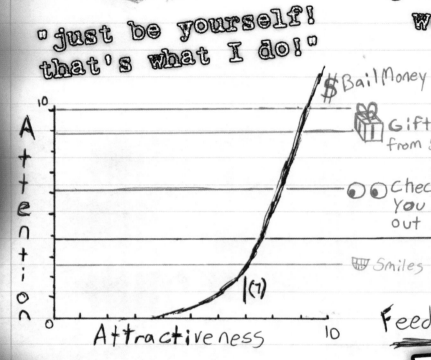

$BailMoney

Gifts from Strangers

Check you out

Feigned Helplesness

Smiles

(7)

Attractiveness

10

Feedback

what women do to show interest changes really fast as you get more attractive.

TRAUMA

trauma can make you think bad is good and good is bad. this girl thinks this guy has problems.

danger

TRAUMA-GNIFICATION

as

Having unresolved Trauma

Can make you see

Healthy people

LEVEL 9 VISUALIZATION

"DOMINANCE" TESTING

Challenger

Current

humans and other mammals have a lot in common. the females test the males for strength.

OK

??

I am going out like this

sometimes, they'll test you even if a challenger isn't there.

if you get tested, the wrong move is to get upset and throw a fit.

Current

Challenger (not present)

-zzzz+

...and if you don't respond, it can turn the test back on her... "why isn't he jealous?"

IF no response...

the right move is to know your boundaries, make it clear what you'll do if they're crossed, and then actually do it.

pay attention to me

TECHNOLOGY + ATTENTION

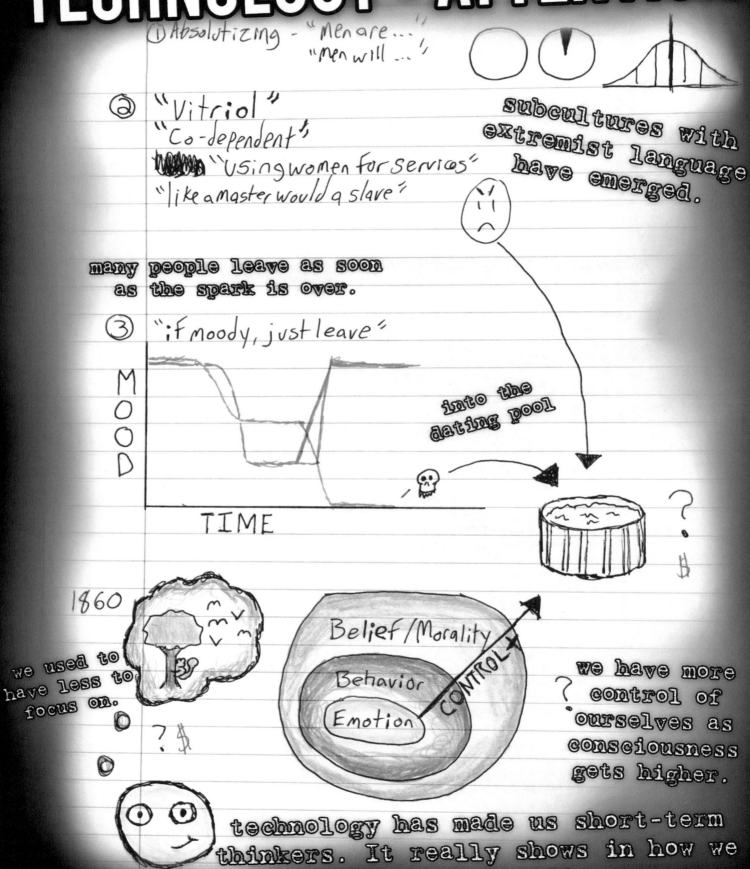

① Absolutizing - "Men are..." "men will ..."

② "Vitriol"
"Co-dependent"
~~XXXX~~ "Using women for services"
"like a master would a slave"

subcultures with extremist language have emerged.

many people leave as soon as the spark is over.

③ "if moody, just leave"

MOOD

TIME

into the dating pool

?
$

1860

we used to have less to focus on.

?
$

Belief/Morality

Behavior

Emotion

CONTROL

we have more control of ourselves as consciousness gets higher.

technology has made us short-term thinkers. It really shows in how we use social media.

MORE LEVELS DEPICTIONS

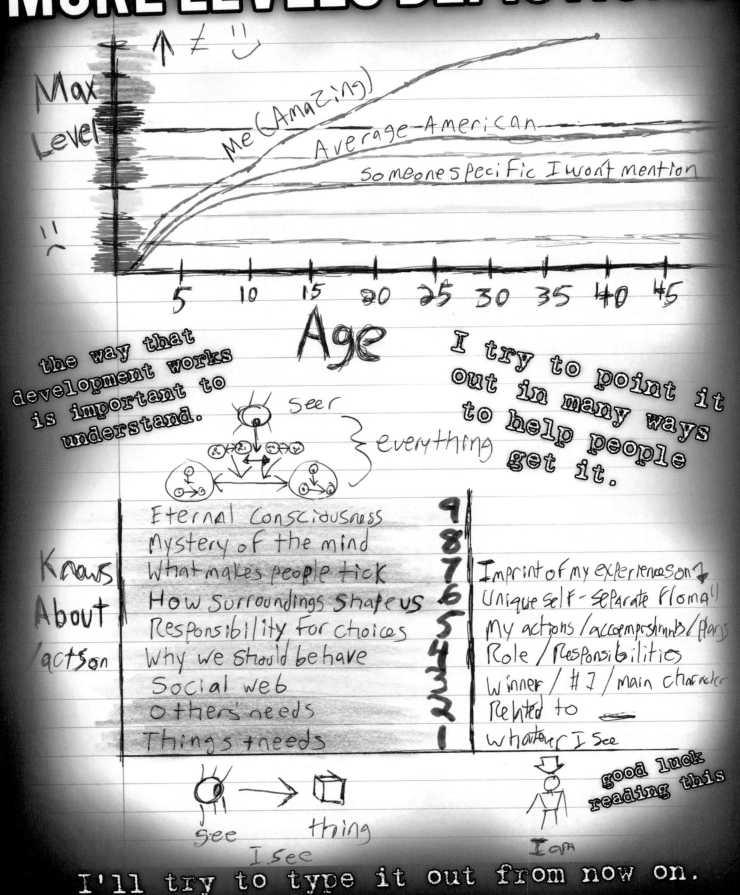

Max Level

Me (Amazing)

Average American

Someone specific I wont mention

5 10 15 20 25 30 35 40 45

Age

the way that development works is important to understand.

seer

} everything

I try to point it out in many ways to help people get it.

Knows About /action		
Eternal Consciousness	9	
Mystery of the mind	8	
What makes people tick	7	Imprint of my experiences on
How surroundings shape us	6	Unique self - separate from all
Responsibility for choices	5	My actions / accomplishments / plans
Why we should behave	4	Role / Responsibilities
Social web	3	Winner / #1 / main character
Others needs	2	Related to ___
Things + needs	1	Whatever I see

see → thing

I see

I am

good luck reading this

I'll try to type it out from now on.

GOOD + BAD CHOICES

I'm disappointed at how many people think relationships need to be constantly fun. making them last means getting through hard times.

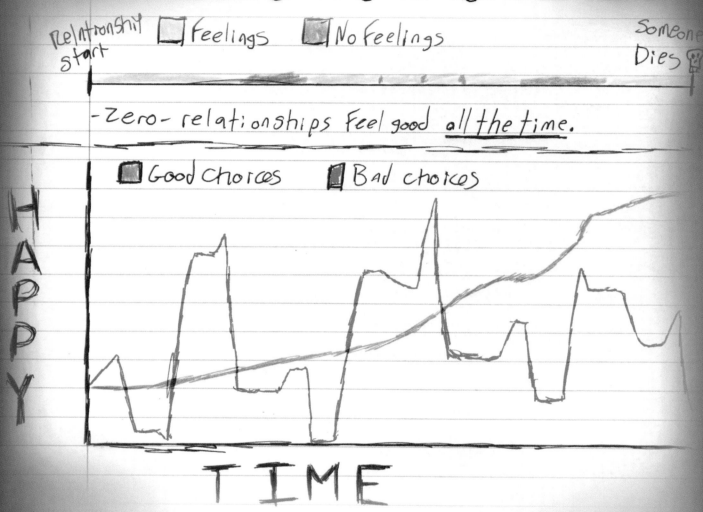

good choices may not be as fun right away, but your life gets better over time.

bad choices might be super fun, but you usually pay for it later.

WoCuDaDeMa

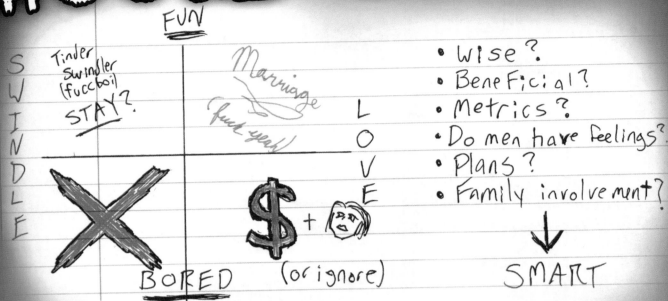

FUN

S W I N D L E	Tinder Swindler (fuccboi) STAY?	Marriage (fuck yeah)

L O V E

- Wise?
- Beneficial?
- Metrics?
- Do men have feelings?
- Plans?
- Family involvement?

↓

X

$ + 😟

SMART

BORED   (or ignore)

some women made their own dating chart where the axes were "fun" and "love."

NOTES: (to keep woman)
- After 3 wk, be rich
- Be money

Da
↓
WoCuDeMa   Don't   Go For it

FUN ↑ +   Reconsider
   ↓ -

SWIND.   LOVE

I helped them out and added "smart" so they could remember to ask themselves if it's a good idea to leave as soon as it's not fun.

the "Women's Cubic Dating Decision Matrix"

OFF CHANCE

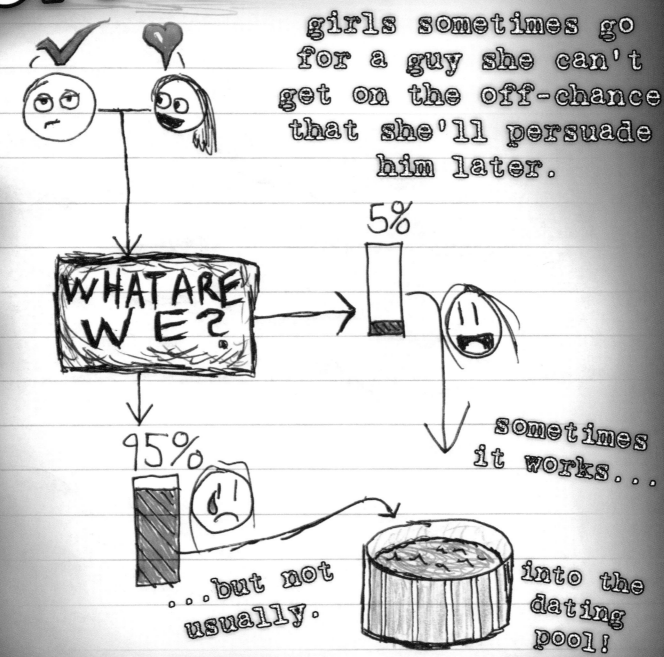

girls sometimes go for a guy she can't get on the off-chance that she'll persuade him later.

5%

WHAT ARE WE?

sometimes it works...

95%

...but not usually.

into the dating pool!

one of the biggest messages I want to get out there is "don't expect the changes you imagined, just take or leave what you're getting."

READING HER MIND

Reading women's minds is a difficult but necessary skill, you have to use your gut feelings. Learn what your guts are telling you about the situation she's showing to you

cursive lol no one can read this anymore

have you ever said 'no' to an invitation, but hoped they would persuade you? maybe you wanted to feel 'extra' invited?

if you remember how that feels, it might help you understand what's going on when women want you to know what they want without telling you.

DIVORCE RATES

statistics are hard to understand.

LESBIAN MARRIAGE + Divorce Rates

I do "light" research (principles are more important to me).

they say that lesbian marriages fail the most, then straight, then gay.

= 72%   = LESS THAN 72% (did not look up)

that can make it seem like women create more relationship problems.

Projection
- Ignored
- Inequality - housework
- Domestic Violence
- Adultery

masculinity has always been considered 'positive' and femininity 'negative...'

$500k -cheesecake Factory

...so maybe it's just a lot of neediness and bad feelings?

all we can really know is what we observe.

there's never one answer for all situations. it's best to keep an open mind.

YOUR TWENTIES

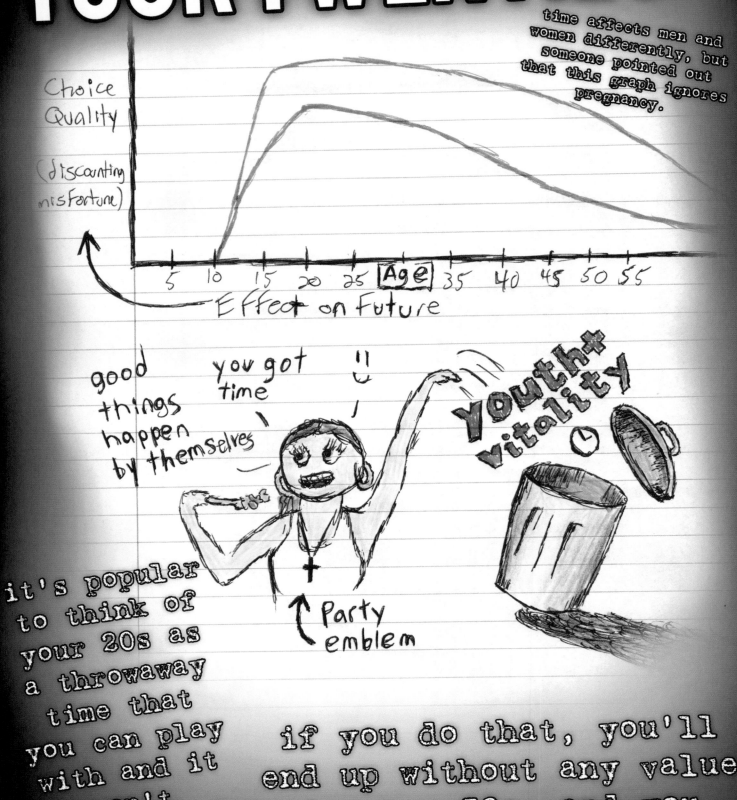

time affects men and women differently, but someone pointed out that this graph ignores pregnancy.

Choice Quality

(discounting misfortune)

5 10 15 20 25 [Age] 35 40 45 50 55

Effect on Future

good things happen by themselves

you got time !!

youth+ vitality

Party emblem

it's popular to think of your 20s as a throwaway time that you can play with and it won't matter.

if you do that, you'll end up without any value in your 30s, and you don't want that.

THE APPROACH

a lot of dating gurus promote "day game," where you approach strange women in public.

how women feel when most men approach

- Subway - trapped
- Check for vendors - that's what you're doing.
- hostage negotiations
- you are th situation
- They are managing you - they have to.
- They do not owe you, but must fear your possible behavior
- Worst case scenario, she dies. Best = you are not fun.

my recommend -ations

Key #1: Distinguish OPTIONAL SOCIAL spaces from spaces of necessity.

Key #2: Distinguish CLEAR INVITATIONS from your fantasies.

Key #3: Women feign interest for their personal safety.

 0.5% NOT DANGER

 X200 =

 hand-kerchief

a good sign

you may not be a danger, but she can't take that chance 200 times.

if you approach strange women in public, you'd better be both good at it and attractive. otherwise, what are you accomplishing?

how women see most of us

ATTENTION-SEEKING

some people will do things they shouldn't do right in front of you and then tell you they aren't really doing them.

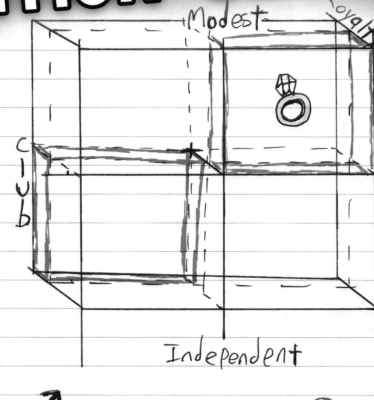

Independent

modest appearance, loyal behavior, and where she spends time are how you should judge the riskiness of her behavior.

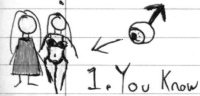

some girls like to get dressed up to get attention and go out drinking...

1. You know men will go for it more.
2. No one is immune to temptation.

...and then they say they're NOT doing it for attention.

learn to trust what you see, not what you hear!

if you believe that, you've been tricked. don't get your mind lost in the "mystery zone," where things "aren't what they look like."

INSTINCTS

ooga booga

The human brain is optimized for hunter-gatherer life.

Birds know how to migrate - instinct.

Caterpillars know how to make a cocoon. Instinct.

most humans forget that they have instincts.

We lived in small tribes outside for a long time.

THREAT

equality means you lose women. fewer babies.

Population

Our ancestors preserved women preferentially over men. That way, more babies per year.

Women have the instinct to stay safe.

Sacrifice Men

Sacrificing men to save women means more babies.

Men have the instinct to rush to stop danger.

(BAD THING)

the way we evolved still influences the way we behave. our brains haven't caught up (and probably never will).

lower- IQ people have more offspring (I'm pretty sure.)

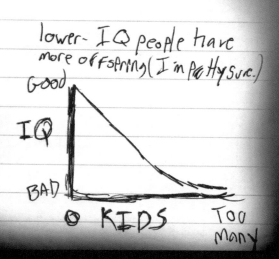

Good

IQ

BAD

0 KIDS Too Many

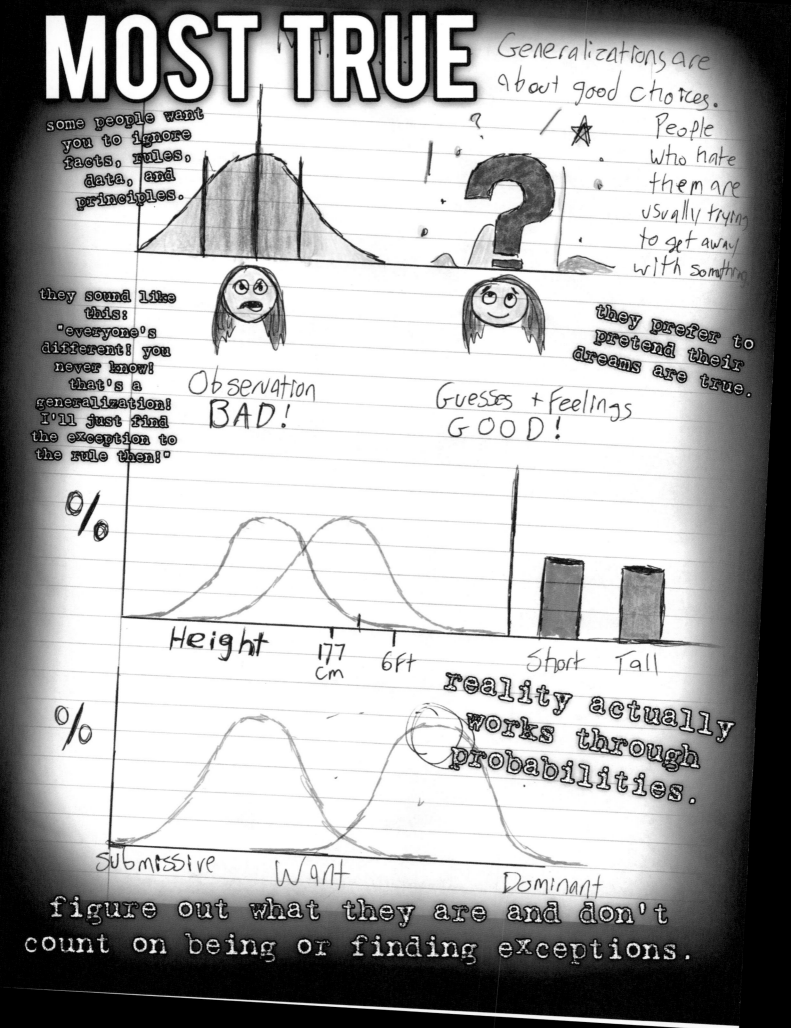

NEXT DOOR WIFE

some lady said that living next door to her husband might help extend the marriage.

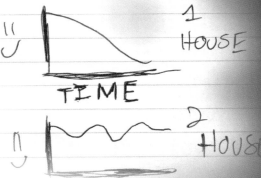

maybe she's right, but in this economy?

MATE CHOICE COPYING

I never thought that girls would like it when I was able to get other girls. I thought they wanted a one-woman man.

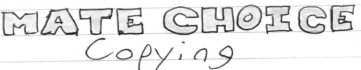

sometimes, when they see you're in demand, they like you even more.

I once got "caught," but she smiled and explained that it made me look even better.

also, look out for snakes and spiders on women, they mean "you might get bitten when you're not looking."

RED FLAGS

we talk about red flags for a reason. don't start relationships with someone who has too many.

(I did, but only because I never had a future until last month)

JESUS

REPENT

some of my fans think religion is bad, but I think we all agree...

the LORD would be aghast at the state of things today.

TRANSACTIONAL

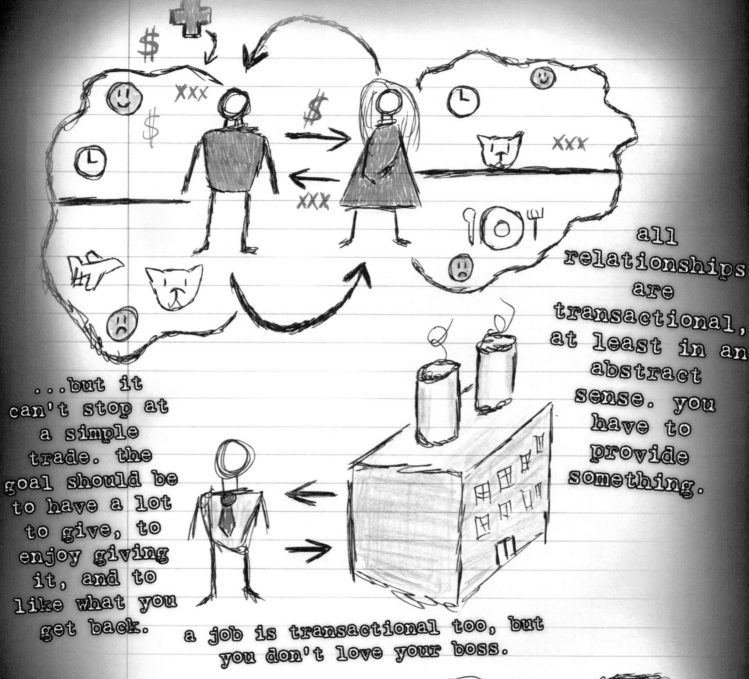

all relationships are transactional, at least in an abstract sense. you have to provide something.

...but it can't stop at a simple trade. the goal should be to have a lot to give, to enjoy giving it, and to like what you get back.

a job is transactional too, but you don't love your boss.

we also give each other meaning, not just stuff.

MOM
(Dad in other state)

SCREAMING AT VEGETABLES

a girl named 'Abby' (why is it always 'Abby?') complained that no one wanted to take her to pumpkin scream time, so I offered.

she said 'yes' in the comments, but didn't follow back. most of these girls just want attention, not to actually meet you.

(see 'basic thirst trap')

Girls who cry about being alone (on Internet)

99.9%

Margin of error: 0.8%

0.1%

Want to

Want

they say "if you put her first, she'll put you last."

WHAT COMES FIRST

no matter how much you like her, don't put her above your life's purpose. if it goes well, and you choose her to be along for the ride, she'll feel like she's first anyway.

some women are even mean to the guys who put them on pedestals.

ANGER MONSTER

SAYING + DOING

it's normal for women to get jealous about other women you know, just don't let it go too far.

don't listen to what people say. watch what they do, and look in their eyes.

(I'm glad I knew how to draw emotions.)

BIRDTEST

a smart way to test how someone feels about you is to talk about a bird (or whatever else is around to talk about).

it's like asking them "do you want to connect with me right now?" this works for long relationships and for meeting someone new.

#1

"I'm so great" vs. "look at that"

it works better than the more direct approach.

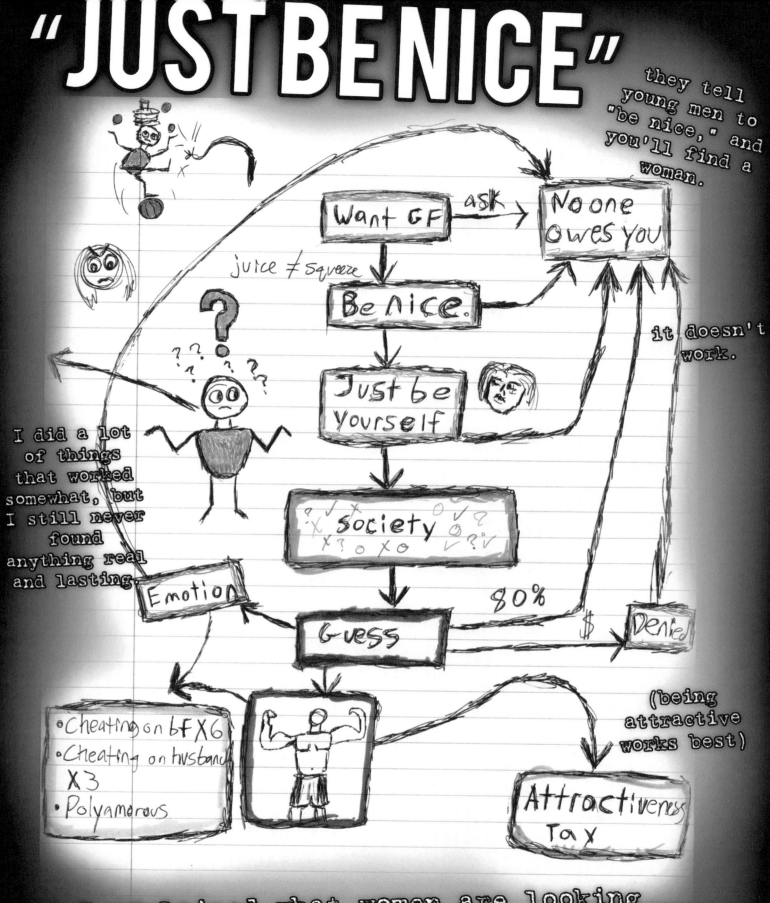

WE LIVE IN A SOCIETY

society isn't really made of people, it's made of relationships. if relationships are weak, society degrades.

Ability to bond

Relationship strength

Ability to bond

Dap 'em UP

some recent trends are weakening relationships.

TIME-TESTED

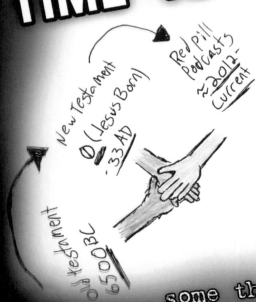

New Testament 0 (Jesus Born) -33 AD

Red pill Podcasts ≈ 2012- current

Old Testament (500 BC)

some things remain true throughout time.

I'm an alpha male! (In the idealized version of myself.)

HERO GAME

BEING

identity is a funny thing. some people say that they 'are' something that they only wish to be.

SEX FIGHT

I argued with Macken Murphy, the world's most prominent horniness analyst.

it's on my YouTube channel. it's called "SEX FIGHT" because I compulsively must ruin everything.

APFUL

APFUL

das ist ein apfel.

GOOD FOR YOU

choices have effects on the future.

FEELS GOOD

"Good"
"nice"
"wise"

"What is it with girls like me?"

I want Fun NOW.

FEELS BAD

"stoic"
"Admirable"
"strong"

yes

"liberal"

VOTE Communism

no

fun is fun, but if you make only fun choices, you'll ruin your life...

GOOD FOR YOU

or for the world

...and if enough people ruin their lives, you ruin the world.

Quality / Time

Quality / Time

KINDS OF LOVE

Eros
Ludus Mania = Fun, young, sexy

Pragma
Storge Agape = Responsible, self-sacrificial, Familial

there are many reasons that people begin and maintain relationships.

I only focus on the fun, popular ones. that's how we form relationships now, so it has the most explanatory power.

PRETTY GIRL PROBLEMS

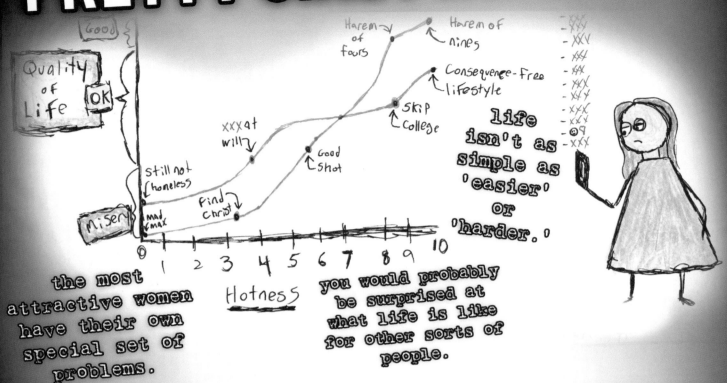

EXPERIENCE + INNOCENCE

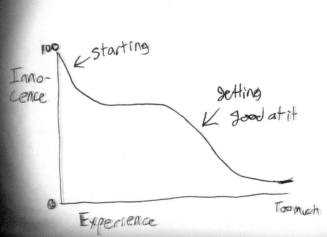

WHERE THE GOOD MEN ARE

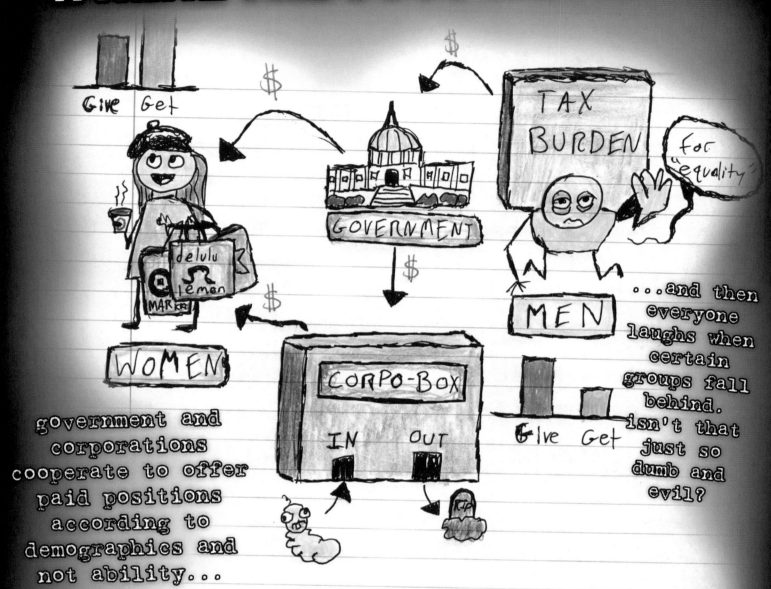

government and corporations cooperate to offer paid positions according to demographics and not ability...

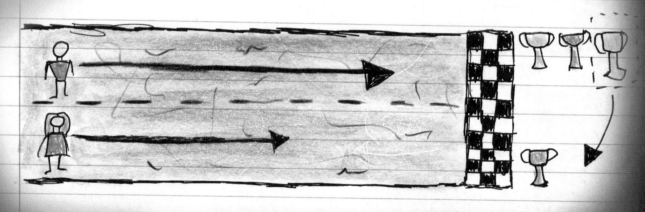

so if life was a race, it's like one group was winning, so everyone else voted to take their trophies, and then said "ha ha, you're losing."

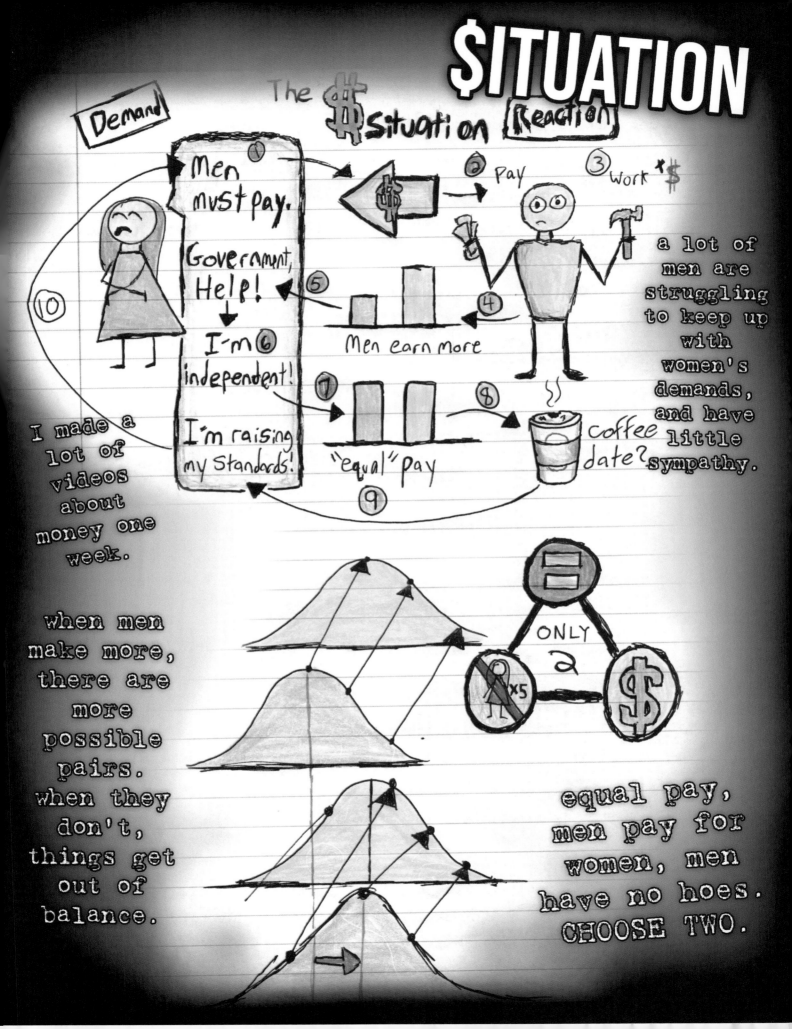

EQUALITY OF WHAT?

I thought we all agreed on equality. so why doesn't that apply to paying?

I think women instinctively want men who have more, but also instinctively want equality. you can't have both, and trying for it causes weird problems.

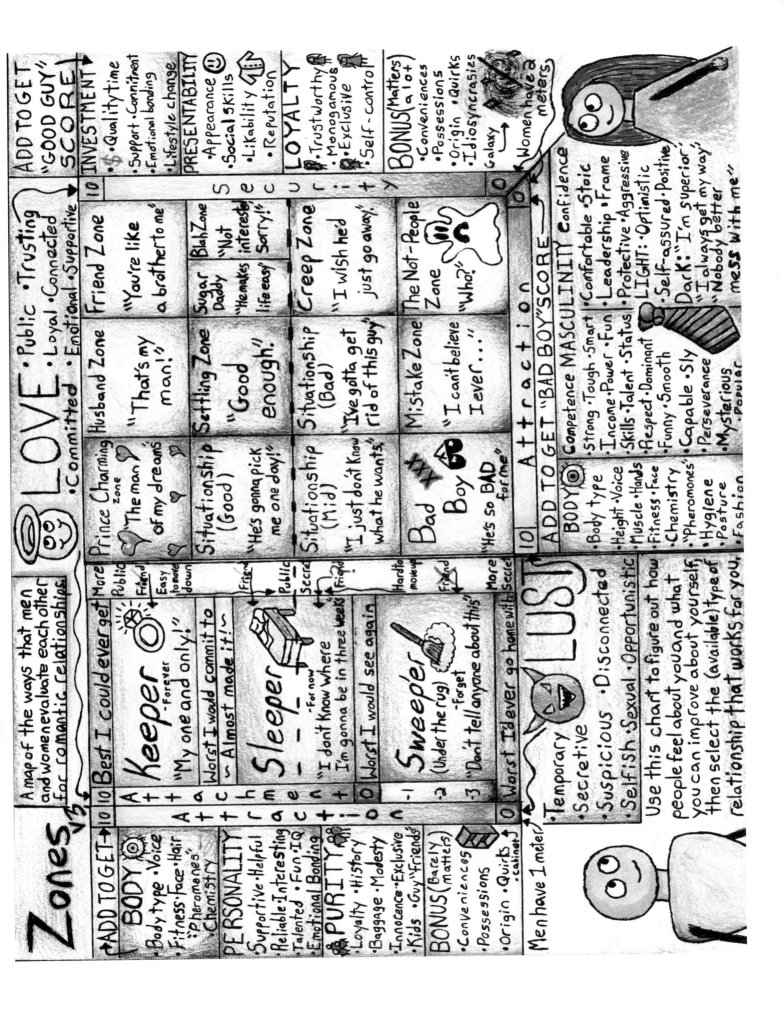

how attractive

"How can I tell how attractive I am?" This was the most common question for hoe_math after the release of Zones v2. "How Attractive?" is the bluntly-named, inward-pointing answer.

In order to know how attractive you are in general, you need to pay attention to how others treat you and how attractive you find them. This requires that you first build the skills of verbal and nonverbal communication, and self-transparency.

You cannot know where you are on the chart without being honest with yourself about how others are treating you. "I think the stripper likes me" is going to keep you in delusion forever, where you'll be missing out on more effective life choices.

"How Attractive?" contains example relationships to illustrate this principle, illustrations of traits that humans find universally, usually, and subjectively attractive, the "Not-People Zone" along with a bell curve to show just how important it is to stand out to the woman of your interest, and a reminder of how much variation there can be in how an individual is perceived by others.

Additionally, there are reminders of how unfamiliar men and women might see each other in modern culture, and written instructions for how to judge others fairly and how to choose partners intelligently.

Most of us experience an immature temptation to see ourselves as being more valuable than we really are. To stay stuck in this delusion might prevent you from feeling the sting of being average (or worse), but it will cause the sting of rejection, broken hearts, loneliness, frustration, and regret.

As much as we are tempted to believe what makes us feel right, powerful, and superior, the actual power of belief only comes from choosing ones that are accurate. You cannot make effective change in the world if you forego its truths for soothing delusions. You must know the map before you travel.

WHAT WOMEN WANT

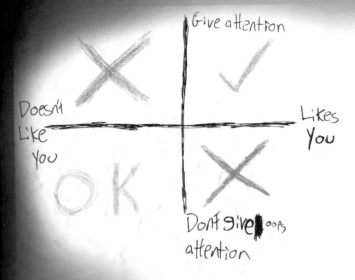

women say they know what they want, but they never seem to tell us. They go "I like attention," and you give her attention, and she goes "EW."

they're not lying... they're just leaving a few things out.

STEALING

Women who will come after you

Chance that women will come after you (monthly)

some girls worry about other girls trying to steal their men.

sometimes they worry too much, and everything begins to look like a reason to cause drama.

1 Day around

28 Days around

CYCLES

male and female hormone cycles change in time with the sun and the moon, so astrology is at least that true.

don't listen to people who tell you we should live more like chimpanzees or bonobos. they never know what they're talking about.

MONKEY NONSENSE

- Individual
- Clear boundaries
- Paternity bound to Provision

- Collective
- Blurry boundaries
- Uncertain Paternity (controlled by Fem.)

♂3 ♀2/1
♂1 ♀2/3
♂1 ♀3

♂1 ♀3
♂3 ♀2/3
♂3 ♀2

♂2 ♀1/2
♂2 ♀1
♂2 ♀1

③ Bonobo Disaster

① Monogamy

Peace: 2
Prosperity: 1

② Polygamy / Polygyny

Peace: 3
Prosperity: 2

we have DNA in common with bananas.

Peace: 1
Prosperity: 3

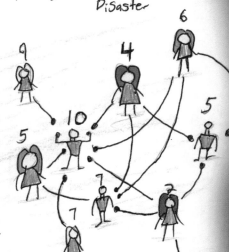

non-monogamy
Bad For: CIVILISATION
good for Female choice

they always say "we have DNA in common with bonobos!" or something idiotic.

"DATA"

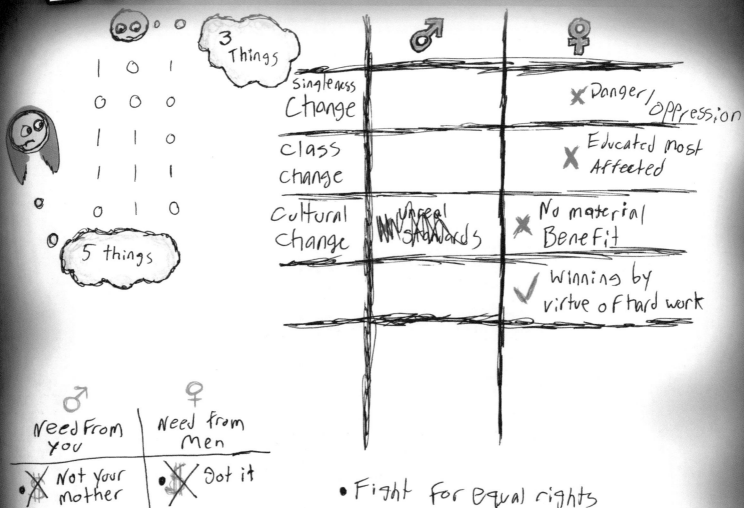

3 Things

1	0	1
0	0	0
1	1	0
1	1	1
0	1	0

5 things

	♂	♀
Singleness Change		✗ Danger / Oppression
Class change		✗ Educated most Affected
Cultural Change	Unreal Standards	✗ No material Benefit
		✓ Winning by virtue of hard work

♂ Need From you	♀ Need from Men
✗ Not your mother	✗ Got it
• Emotional support not your therapist	• Emotional support

- Fight for equal rights
- Vote for economic privilege
- Reject men with "no material benefit"
- Demand support, offer none
- Label men "dangerous"

the way this girl told her story "based on the data" was really just an opinion with numbers near it.

I offered her a very different story, which she ignored.

CHEATING STYLES

men and women cheat differently. men usually go for the easy target who's less attractive, and women usually go for the "upgrade."

DIFFERENT SKILLS

it's important to have skills, but different skills have different effects on different women. choose carefully!

GHOSTING

ghosting hurts people's feelings, and those feelings go right back into the dating pool, which you're still in.

$$\frac{Ghosted}{Ghosting} = Err/inf$$

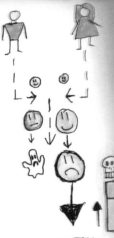

cart corral

Where the F*** ever I want!

RESPOND TO MOLLY

DEATH PENALTY

NO 1/8" headphone jack

DATING POOL

NEGOTIATIONS

relationships are an ongoing negotiation.

many people think that once you find someone, you're done. actually, that's where the real work starts.

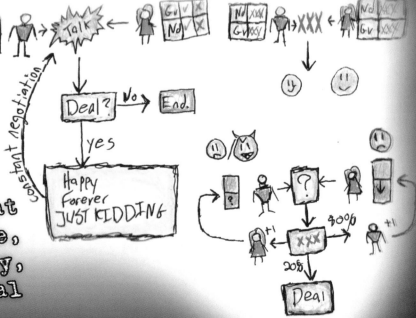

Talk

constant negotiation

Deal? → No → End.

yes

Happy Forever JUST KIDDING

Deal

ABUNDANCE MENTALITY

some women get mad in advance about what it feels like you might be doing.

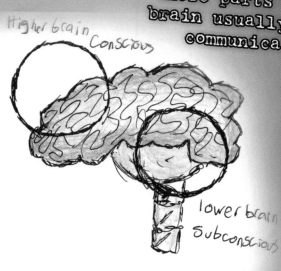

these parts of the brain usually don't communicate.

Higher brain Conscious

lower brain Subconscious

if she likes you until you like her back, she might have just liked the idea of winning you from other girls.

What she doesn't see | What she sees

be conscious of what people can and can't see about you.

one of the most confusing things about women: they like you more when you have a lot of girls around you, but they also get mad when they think you're communicating with them.

that was hoe_math.

Go now and walk the path.

Printed in Great Britain
by Amazon

40163433R00062